FIND YOUR VOICE

28 Secrets To Inspire You To Speak Up

ROBERT KENNEDY III

ISBN: 1-7321890-2-7

ISBN-13: 978-1-7321890-2-7

DEDICATION

There's no question. This is a standing dedication. My amazing and lovely wife, Nadia, you mean so much to me. You speed me up and you slow me down. You allow me to be who I am and keep me from being who I shouldn't be.

People call me RK3. But, I wouldn't be the third without the first. Grandpa Robert just recently passed away at 104 years of pure genius and compassion. He was such an inspiration and I loved him a great deal.

Grandpa, thanks for your example. You're a big reason for my voice.

LOOKING FOR THE IDEAL PROFESSIONAL SPEAKER FOR YOUR NEXT EVENT?

If you love when your audience or your employees are energized, laughing and inspired, then you need to hire Robert Kennedy III for your next keynote or workshop training.

"Robert's natural ability to bring joy and excitement into a room is like no other. He was authentic, informative and fun. We received glowing reviews from attendees about his performance. One of the best choices we made was choosing Robert for our event." - K. O'Connor - University of Maryland

"I've had the pleasure of scheduling speakers for 6+ years. Robert's presentation is among the few that attendees continuously rave about." - K. Leonard - Small Business University

"This was REALLY good. It was fun, energetic, LOUD!! Wow! We don't get to do this as staff that often...be ourselves for a minute. We will definitely bring him back." - T. Frett, VP, NeighborWorks America

TO CONTACT OR BOOK ROBERT (RK3) TO SPEAK:

RK3 International

14625 Baltimore Ave. #357

Laurel, MD 20707

410-575-3657

speaking@robertkennedy3.com

www.robertkennedy3.com

www.kennetikkommunications.com

Introduction

You're phenomenal! Has anyone told you that lately? It's true. You are! The problem is most people don't believe it. Even worse, they believe the problems they face in life are because they're not good enough. Most people don't believe they're worth it. So, they accept mediocre or less. Then, they look at the lives of others through TV or social media thinking, "if only I had more money, all my problems would disappear."

Money gives you access to a different level of life, but it doesn't erase problems. And, most of the lives you see people living online aren't real. So, I've got news for you today, my friend! Your life has happened for a reason! There's purpose behind every moment in your life! Did you have to experience all of them? Maybe not. Some life experiences are created by the choices we make. But, there are many we have no control over.

Control or no control, you have lived each moment and you can use each moment. Each moment contains a snippet of the story you're building. This story is your personal, unique code to influence and impact. The more you use this story, the more authentic you'll be and the more connected to people you can become.

My job with this book is to encourage, empower and inspire you to move past the shame in your story. It's time to turn up the volume on your life because someone needs to hear it! Your story is yours because you're living it. But, someone else needs to hear it so they can truly begin living theirs.

Every quote in this book was chosen with you in mind. Every reflection was written to help you SPEAK UP! Every word was crafted to help you UNLEASH your power and FIND YOUR VOICE!

Read this, then LIVE it!

Find some additional resources to help you FIND YOUR VOICE at
www.robertkennedy3.com/findyourvoice

#1

"The one thing that you have that nobody else has is you. Your voice, your mind, your story, your vision. So write and draw and build and play and dance and live as only you can."

– Neil Gaman

I used to think I had to have an amazing story of tragedy for anyone to listen or care. I didn't come from abject poverty. I've never been homeless (at least not to this point). My limbs all work and I haven't had a tragic accident to shift my entire perspective on life. I'm grateful but it's still so easy to get down on yourself when you live in a world where it seems drama gets all the attention.

Isn't that crazy? You have a good life but you can get sad because your life isn't bad enough? That's just backwards…isn't it?

When you're living your life, it can feel like it's not special and no one else will understand. But, I can guarantee there are experiences you've had that are amazing to others. For example, when I was 8, I taught myself to ride a bike in 30 minutes. I've never thought it was a big deal until recently when I told the story. The short version is I was staying with a friend's family for a few days and had no one to push me or help me learn to balance. So, I figured out how to balance while coasting down the driveway into my friend's garage. Once I felt confident balancing, I pedaled and turned. After 30 minutes, I took my act to the streets. Soon, I was riding with so much confidence you'd never know I'd just learned.

Why didn't I ever tell this particular story? I'd forgotten about it. There was no particular significance to it in my mind. It was just one of those things I'd done. It was regular. It wasn't special. Or, so I thought! But, the moment I shared it during one of my workshops, someone squealed, "Wow, that's a great story!"

Here I was, carrying around something amazing, and yet I thought it was just average.

It's like that for you. You've done amazing things but since you're living your life, you don't always recognize them. But, I'll bet if you were to review the experiences of your life, you'd be able to find something phenomenal. Maybe you don't think it's fantastic initially. Here's how you figure it out. Tell the story. Share it with someone. Use your voice! Their responses will tell you all you need to know. I'll bet you will find a hidden gem or two, right there in a hidden compartment of your memory box.

It's time to open it up!

#2

"Don't you dare, for one more second, surround yourself with people who are not aware of the greatness you are."

– Jo Blackwell-Preston

"You talk too much."

"You ask too many questions!"

"You should be a lawyer because you talk so much!"

I was two or three years old. But, I clearly remember hearing those words.

My mom was a teacher and my dad a minister. They functioned like most parents and sometimes had to leave me in the care of a sitter or family member. They weren't aware of these comments. To be honest, I'm not sure how they would've known. They noticed I was quieter and more reserved. But, it's hard to know what triggers a child to act differently. People used the word "shy."

Around my immediate family, I spoke, laughed and appeared comfortable. But the words used by babysitters, caretakers and even some extended family had their effect. I'm sure they meant well, but, they weren't aware of what their words did. As a child, I didn't understand how to express my feelings so I thought, "Maybe they're right."

Essentially, my voice was muffled because I was still learning how to use it and others didn't understand it. I didn't have a choice in who I surrounded myself with at that age. But, I recognize the impact of that time.

Maybe you've heard similar words. As you think about your life, maybe you've recognized moments where your innate greatness was stifled. Most of us have those moments. But sometimes we hang on to them and use them as reasons for not STEPPING IN.

STEPPING IN is hard and scary. It feels like everything is shaking and nothing is secure. When you finally acknowledge greatness, it can feel like the world, as you know it, is about to flip like an old mattress. There are no guarantees and you don't know how it will turn out.

That's why it's important to surround yourself with people who recognize their own greatness, have activated it, and who can support you in yours.

Their greatness may not match up with yours pound for pound. But, if they're threatened by your greatness, then they're not your support system. Move away from those relationships and search for people who see greatness in you. Look for people who see the impact you can make and who will actively help you move towards the full manifestation of the greatest you.

Be willing to do the same for them. Actively look for others behind you on the journey. Then, help them recognize their own "awesomeness".

#3

"Picture yourself in a living room having a chat with your friends. You would be relaxed and comfortable talking to them, the same applies when public speaking."

– Richard Branson

Watching a great public speaker work is both inspiring and scary. They seem at ease, slinging words back and forth, smiling, grimacing and pulling at your emotional strings. Their words inspire you but the thought of them standing in front of all those people trying to remember all their lines FRIGHTENS YOU.

I'm 8 years old and I'm giving my first public speech. It's children's day at my church and I've been "volun-told" to be one of the speakers for the day. As I stand up, I realize there are over 1200 pairs of eyes staring at me. No one prepares you for that. It's surreal. It happens in slow motion and the camera slowly pans around the room. Some eyes are looking at me expectantly. Others are looking right through me into my soul.

I'm doing everything I can to remove the lump in my throat. I swallow, open my eyes wider and take a deep breath. I twitch my nose. None of it is working...until I begin to speak. The first few sentences are time altering. But, once I find my groove, it's over.

After it ended, I vowed never to speak in front of people AGAIN! But, years later, I recognize the one important result I'd missed. I...WAS...ALIVE! The speech didn't kill me. My friends were still my friends. My parents were still my parents and my world still existed. In fact, my friends were in the audience that day. What if I'd focused on them? What if I'd simply acted as if I was talking to them?

I imagined the conversations and circles of laughter with my friends. Stories floated through my mind and the more I allowed them to float, the more real they became. These stories make you feel like your life is about to end. But, that's not the truth at all. The truth was my friends barely made mention of the speaking. A few said, "good job, Bobby." And, when they did, I knew they were looking up to me with respect instead of looking down on me with mockery as my mind had imagined. The truth was the grown-ups in my world all gushed over the day and I don't know if they remembered any words I said. They just knew it was the opening of my destiny to become a preacher like my dad (that didn't happen).

My point here? I'd made up a lot of stories and none of them came true. And, you may be making up a lot of stories. You may be telling yourself it's too late for you to tell your story. You may be telling yourself no one wants to hear what you have to say. You may even be telling yourself you will fail and fall on your face if you attempt to tell your story. But, that's not the real story.

The real story is where you make it through. The real story is where you come out a winner. The real story is where you grow no matter what happens.

Embrace the real story!

#4

"Your voice is assigned to someone specific. There are certain messages they can only hear from you."

– RK3

As a science teacher I remember explaining physics concepts to my students. Every year, as we explored the concepts, something interesting happened. I called it the 'They-Can't-Hear-Me' event. You see, I would explain a concept in the best way I could, attempting to cover every detail while making it simple and relevant. Yet, there was always a student who would timidly raise their hand saying, "I don't get it, Mr. K."

OK. No problem. "Let's look at this another way."

We'd explore another example or two. Then, the student would respond, "I still don't get it Mr. K."

"Hmm. OK. Let's try it a third way."

This was followed by, "I'm still not getting it, Mr. K."

Every year, without fail, another student would saunter across the classroom to sit next to the student having the problem. They would start out, "Well, here's how you do it..." The new 'student teacher' would then begin to point into different areas of the book or begin writing on paper in order to explain the problem. In many cases, they used the EXACT words I had just finished using and for some odd reason, the light bulb turned on for the other student.

"Ohhhhhhhh, I get it now."

Wow! What was the problem with MY explanation? Different frequency. They just couldn't hear me. For them to get the message, they needed to hear it from a specific voice.

It's the same for you. You have a story to tell and knowledge to share with the world. It might feel like you have nothing important to say because to you, your experiences are normal. I know the feeling. Many times, I have looked at other speakers, presenters, preachers, teachers and trainers and it seemed like they all had amazing stories. I would ask myself, "What do I have to share that would be remotely interesting?"

or, "Why would people listen to me anyway?"

Each person has a unique experience and an important message to share. Some ears will only hear the message from your voice. So, when you hide or give in to the fear of criticism, you're withholding possibility from someone else.

They're out there waiting to hear from you. The time is now for you to speak up and speak out.

#5

"When we speak, we are afraid our words will not be heard or welcomed. When we are silent, we are still afraid. So, it is better to speak."

– Audre Lorde

You've heard quotes and stories about the fear of public speaking, right? Some imagine a stage but many people are afraid of speaking up in conversations and meetings. Why?

The introverts of the world, like myself, may not speak up because it takes energy. When we speak out, this prompts a discourse and we'd rather keep it short and simple. Long conversations and long speeches are our Kryptonite...or at least they feel like it. This even showed up in my writing. I wanted to get straight to the point.

During my freshman year of college, I was in an honors English class. My professor, Ms. Leonard, assigned us essays every week. For the first 4 or 5 weeks, I would go to the computer lab to get my essay typed and turned in. When I received the grade, it was a C or a C+. I remember getting upset because I compared my work to my classmates and their work seemed...well...fluffy. They said the same thing I did, except they seemed to use a lot more words. I got straight to the point. But, this only got me a C. Finally, I learned to set the stage with my writing, warm things up and be a little more "fluffy."

I remember Ms. Leonard's smile when she returned the essay with the first A on the top. I smiled too but it took work. It's like that for many people. Maybe it's like that for you. Speaking up, saying more, being "fluffy" takes energy and it is hard work. For others, there's the fear of not having the correct answer. Then, there are those who don't want to seem unprepared.

When you don't speak, you limit the possibility for change. Speaking alone doesn't cause change. However, it plants the seeds of action. When you stay silent, the world goes on as it did before, spinning the same stories of dissatisfaction. This status quo keeps everyone comfortable even if the comfort is hurting you.

So, it becomes a matter of choosing the discomfort you want. Would you rather experience pain for no reason, or pain for possibility? Ask yourself what you want. Then, decide what change you want to make.

Today is your day to speak up and speak out!

#6

"Stop living like you're scared of being discovered. Instead, speak like the sun needs you in order to shine."

— RK3

Early in my speaking career I encountered a woman who, at the time, led a volunteer organization we'll call "Volunteer Inc." Let's call her "Barb". Barb was leading a meeting of the leaders of Volunteer Inc. She was opinionated and spoke with conviction about where the group should focus. I was in the room to present an idea for a campaign they were about to release. My presentation went well. However, I focused on Barb and how she navigated the conversation and contributions of other leaders who were both younger and older than she was.

Several months later, I was invited to do a technical workshop for another company. As I began the workshop, I noticed the Barb sitting in the back. We smiled with recognition. However, over the course of the day, I noticed she was a bit more reserved. It was as if she was intentionally attempting to camouflage who she was amongst this crew. At lunch, we walked to the company cafeteria where I mentioned my observations. She lightly dismissed my thoughts as her being a bit tired and tense.

Shortly after the workshop, I received an email from Barb. She requested a phone call, stating she had a few big decisions she was pondering and needed some coaching.

Once we hopped on the call, Barb immediately spoke about the tension she was having at work. She was on several projects that tanked. She wasn't the leader for the projects but was very clear on the specific reasons for the projects' failure. They came back to leadership. When I asked why she didn't speak up, she shared a story about the time she did. It led to tension between her and a boss and she wasn't confident in resolving it without losing her job. She was the breadwinner in her family and her job was important. Yet, she regularly felt conflicted because she knew her trepidation kept her department in a tailspin.

Because this is a short book, I'll skip to the end of the call. Ultimately, Barb realized she was making herself sick because she was squeezing her mouth shut. She was doing this because she was nervous about conflict. However, her greatest revelation was her fear of speaking up, taking on a responsibility, and failing. She would then be looked at as a fraud. So, she kept quiet to keep her leadership skills, or lack thereof from being "discovered."

Barb called me recently to let me know how tired she was of squeezing her voice and getting sick. She was so sick of being sick, tired, and tense that she finally spoke up during a meeting where she offered a solution to the projects that were flopping. Everyone sat quiet for a few moments after she spoke. Then an executive, higher than her boss asked, "Why haven't you said anything about this before? You should be leading this project. Come see me after this meeting!"

It's time for you to stop being the world's best kept secret. Some things won't happen the way they're supposed to if you don't speak up. The world needs you! Your story deserves a stage!

#7

"A man who wants to lead the orchestra must turn his back on the crowd."

– Max Lucado

Judgment! We judge others so we're afraid of being judged. It's a natural human behavior. We look at the energy, body language and facial expressions of others and make judgments about how we want to interact with them. We get nervous about what others think of us. Most of us don't want to be singled out as different. We're built for camaraderie and inclusion. Standing on our own is scary because it's lonely.

In 2009, at the age of 12, Malala Yousafzai began writing a blog protesting against the Taliban control in her area in Pakistan and limiting the rights of women. She wrote about unfair treatment and education being stripped away. She penned thoughts about violence and the climate of fear under which they were forced to live.

Initially, she wrote under a pseudonym, but receiving recognition for the blog, her identity was revealed. She was nominated for awards, invited to speak for different audiences and soon her increased profile made her a target for the Taliban.

In October of 2012, while Malala was at school, a masked gunman entered the school and shot her in the head. Amazingly, Malala survived, but she was in critical condition. She was in a coma for several weeks and her father began to prepare her family for her passing. However, by late October, she came out of her coma and began responding well to treatment. By early-January of 2013, she was released from the hospital and moved to a safe place to continue her recovery.

The Islamic clerics in Pakistan were incensed at the Taliban's attempt to assassinate a school girl and issued a fatwa, or formal ruling, against the Taliban. A petition issued in Malala's name received more than 2 million signatures and included the following requests:

- We call on Pakistan to agree to a plan to deliver education for every child.

- We call on all countries to outlaw discrimination against girls.

- We call on international organisations to ensure the world's 61 million out-of-school children are in education by the end of 2015.

Malala's fight was taken to the United Nations where she spoke in July of 2013, less than a year after her shooting. She still speaks today about the rights of young girls to have education and was awarded the Nobel Peace Prize in 2014.

In most cases, the response to your words will not be as severe as it was for Malala. But, I admit, this fear makes it difficult to speak up.

In spite of the fear, sometimes you have an idea that must be shared. It might be a world changing story, but, you won't know until you open your mouth. You may be scared, but it's time for you to close your eyes and jump. It'll be okay. You must believe. Every great entrepreneur, actor, president, prime minister or leader decided to jump. Sure, some have failed. But, many succeeded. You know their names. You see them. It's time for you to be one of them!

#8

"When you hide your story, you're denying someone the very tool they need to overcome their obstacle."

— RK3

I wanted to start a business, so I searched "Alta Vista" and "Ask Jeeves."

If you don't recognize those names, you were born after 1998. Those were the search engines back before Google was synonymous with online search.

I tapped into my keyboard, "starting a business." When the results came back, I clicked the top link, "5 Steps To Starting Your Business."

After downloading the paperwork from the IRS, I searched the appropriate registry for my business name. Finally, I got the forms necessary to submit my name with my payment.

Once the approved paperwork arrived, I remember the feeling. I wanted to dance on the ceiling. I was official! I was a business. This was real!

But, what if I didn't have the roadmap? Could I have started and registered the business without the information I found online? Maybe! Sure, I could have asked questions or gone to the library.

But, the process was so much easier because I found an article that listed the process step by step.

It's just like that for you. You're the search engine, and your life is the story. Someone is looking for information on getting past their current challenges. You are THEIR Google. Maybe you feel like this is a lot of pressure. I've been telling you to live life on your terms, yet here I am, telling you someone else needs you.

The truth is we are all connected. When you to live a copy of someone else's life, it fails. It fails because it isn't authentic. It fails because it is not organic. But, it also doesn't happen in isolation. You need other people, and they need you. They need to see you living your story, and they also benefit from hearing you speak about your story. This is how they create their roadmap.

Imagine typing keywords into a search engine and receiving no response. This is what it's like when you refuse to share your story. Someone is tapping away, trying to find the answer to their problem. And you've got it!

Share it!

#9

"Communication is merely an exchange of information, but connection is an exchange of our humanity."

– Sean Stephenson

Joni was three years old when a new family moved in next door. They were from Poland, and the parents spoke broken-English. Their son, Michael, was also three and didn't speak English at all. A few days after moving in, Michael was playing outside on the front porch when he spied Joni staring at him through the fence. Their eyes met, and Joni immediately walked past the fence. She was soon standing directly in front of Michael.

She waved hello, and Michael waved back. After a few moments of silence, Joni grabbed Michael's hand and guided him over to the swing set in the yard. Soon, both children were laughing and giggling loudly as if they'd known each other for years.

By the end of the summer, Michael spoke near-perfect English, and Joni knew quite a few words in Polish.

How were they able to understand each other and play together so quickly? First, they had the desire to play with each other. Second, they viewed the language difference as an opportunity instead of a barrier. They were creative. They pointed. They played charades. They did whatever it took to understand and be understood without judgment.

They stepped past communication to connection!

As I grew up in New York City, I constantly came in contact with people who spoke languages other than English. For years, we noticed the accents and the difficulty some had with English. But, I never recognized they were "forced" to speak English. What if I had to learn their language or find a different way to communicate other than spoken language? In the city, we had "options." If you didn't understand someone, you just went somewhere else. But, options removed the connection.

It's tempting to think about communication as speaking or writing. It IS those things. But it's so much more. And this becomes even more obvious when we face a situation where languages are different. We aren't FORCED to communicate with each other, so, quite often, we choose the easier path.

We place communication before connection. But, what if we valued connection more? What if connecting was our first goal?

#10

"Self-confidence is the
memory of success."

– David Story

I hopped into my car, turned the key and, without thinking, checked my mirrors. Before I knew it, my right foot pressed the gas pedal, and the car was rolling down the street. Nothing prompted it but my mind then scrolled back to the day my dad gave me the keys and said, "Hop in" gesturing toward the driver's side.

I'd never driven before so excitement and fear both grabbed me while my mind filled with questions...

"What if I crash?"

"How do I turn a corner?"

"What gear do I use and when do I use it?"

"What if it goes too fast?"

The flood of thoughts consumed me. Then, I heard my dad's voice, "Just put the key in and turn it. I'll guide you through the rest."

Hearing his voice reassured and calmed me. He talked me through every step slowly and I completed the lesson without a scratch.

After a few lessons, I was a pro.

That's how confidence works. You aren't born with it. Confidence is developed after courage. Once you act and achieve, then it's easier to be sure of yourself. So, if you lack confidence in a specific area, the best way to develop it is to do something.

This is how it is with your voice. Mentally, you aren't always sure what to say. You hold back because you aren't sure how it will be received. And it isn't just you. For years, I held back my own voice. I came up with many excuses.

"I'm an introvert."

"I don't have anything new to say."

"They've heard this all before. What I have to say isn't that brilliant."

These stories, while true in some ways, kept me from finding the one thing I needed in order to truly shine…my voice.

So, in order to move forward, I had to act. I decided I would no longer sit in the background and wait to be called. I gathered my courage and began to tell my story.

It's the same for you. Go for it!

Self-confidence comes only after ACTION!

#11

"What we say is important because in most cases, what the mouth speaks, the heart is full of."

– Jim Beggs

Complainers complain. Whiners whine! Gossipers gossip! What comes out of your mouth is what you are. We don't think about it that way because most people don't speak one way all the time. However, we have an aura or general energy about us. You become known for how you speak.

If a reporter asked your friends to describe you in 1-3 words, what would they say? Well, they are your friend so they would say something nice. But, would they use words like positive, uplifting, optimistic, service-oriented, or would they say nice, cool person or always there? What POWER words would they use to describe you?

Several years ago, I read Living Forward by Michael Hyatt and Daniel Harkavy. In the book, they asked a question I have never forgotten. "At your funeral, what would people say about you?"

They went on to write about the process of preparing your own eulogy. This is hard for many people because most of us don't want to think about dying. But, the hard fact is that many people don't think about living. When you can take a good look at your life, you can do something about it. You move from just taking what life gives you to creating an intentional reality. You move from silently complying with life's whims to actively speaking your intent and executing. Your life is being recorded anyway and one day people will play back the recording from their own perspective. At that point, you can do nothing to change their narrative.

If you can write out your own eulogy, the words you would WANT people to say about you, then it becomes much easier to intentionally create it in your life. People define us by the things we do but, also by what we say.

This is good news. We can control it. You can choose what comes out of your mouth. It isn't an involuntary action. You're in charge! So, what are you going to do with this power?

Imagine your heart is a soft ketchup bottle. Whatever you fill it with comes out when you squeeze. So, if you fill it with gratitude, when squeezed, gratitude goodness comes out. If you fill it with positive affirmations, when squeezed, perpetual positive comes out.

Now, your job is to find the "stuff" to fill your bottle because at some point, it will be squeezed.

#12

"Don't wait until everything is just right. It will never be perfect. There will always be challenges, obstacles and less than perfect conditions. So what? Get started now. With each step you take, you will grow stronger and stronger, more and more skilled, more and more self-confident and more and more successful."

– Mark Victor Hansen

Wait! Wait! I'm not ready yet!

Have you heard those words coming from your mouth? Those are the words of procrastination and delay. We say them often. Instead of starting today, we say, "I'll start on Sunday so it's easier for me to track with the weeks." or

"I need to wait until I feel more ready." or

"I'm just too busy right now. I need to wait until my schedule lightens up a bit."

Are those valid reasons? Sure. But perfect conditions rarely, if ever, exist.

I'm guilty. Several years ago, I decided to focus on my health. And like many people at the time, I decided to invest in a program called P90x. If you have never heard of it, P90x is a fitness program developed by trainer, Tony Horton, and distributed through the company, Beachbody. The concept of this program is committing to a workout program every day for 90 days. This would get you ripped, lean and in shape. I looked into the mirror to assess my body. It wasn't an overweight body, but I wanted to get RIPPED! So, I committed and invested.

When the box came, I ripped it open and eagerly went through the pages of the booklet which accompanied the DVDs. In addition to the video material and booklet, there was a calendar. I carefully unfolded it and went to my intended workout area in the basement where I carefully attached it to the wall.

"Ninety days. That's doable. I'm ready.", I thought.

Then, I looked at my calendar and noticed it was the 23rd of the month.

"Hmmm, that's an odd start date. I need a round number. That will make this so much easier. I'll wait until the first."

Then, I placed the DVDs on a shelf near to the TV and didn't think about them again for another 2 weeks. One day, I happened to be in the basement, saw the DVDs and noticed the calendar on the wall.

"Wow, I missed the first. I should really do this." So, I picked up the booklet again and began exploring the workouts a bit. Some were an hour and others were 90 minutes. I took particular notice of one that was close to 90 minutes but also asked you to do a 15 minute ab workout right after.

"Ummm, that's a long time."

This went on for a few weeks until one day I happened upon the receipt and noticed I had now purchased the product 5 months earlier. WOW! What happened to the time?

It happens to the best of us. We delay because we want things to be easy…just right…close to perfect…convenient. But life rarely works like that.

It's up to you. Decide what you want. Decide when you want it and go for it. The longer you wait, the longer it takes to reach the goal and the less likely you'll do it. What call do you need to make today? What email do you need to send? Who can get you on a stage to share your story? It's time to ACT! That's it! ACTION!

#13

"If your life was perfect, then your story wouldn't be interesting."

— RK3

Kal-El's parents decided it was time to explore other worlds. So, they carefully prepared a pod, included enough sustenance for 20 days and sent Kal-El on his way. He landed in a cornfield where a kind family found him and took him in.

They treated him as their own and sent him to school every day. He showed an interest in journalism and worked as a reporter for his school newspaper. After going to college, he became a reporter for the Daily Planet where he met his wife, Lois. They had 3 children and lived happily ever after.

What did you think? Was the story interesting? You read it but you wouldn't rent it if it were a movie. There were no plot twists, no drama, nothing to make you sit up and pay attention. If you noticed, there wasn't even a Superman because there was no need for one.

I remember thinking no one would ever want to hear my story because it wasn't interesting enough. I had never been hit by a drunk driver. I was blessed enough to be born with all my limbs. My health was great and doctor visits were not frequent, other than the check-ups every year. While my family wasn't rich growing up, we always had food and never went to bed hungry. I don't ever remember being without a vehicle. My parents went to school and were professionals in their chosen fields. Life was good...so good, no one would want to hear about it, right? Reality TV makes money and catches eyeballs because of how drama-filled it is. My life had some moments but nothing to make anyone pop-up and pay attention. This was what I thought.

And I'm not the only one who has thought this way. Many of you reading this have had this same thought. Because you have felt this way, your story has been internalized and untold. The truth is none of us have perfect lives. But, most of us want to hide the moments of imperfection. We don't want to look bad...unless we're getting paid or there is some more significant benefit that exceeds the embarrassment.

A perfect life is an uninteresting and uninspiring life. If you want to speak and inspire others, then you're asking for drama...tales of conquest. So, when the unexpected happens, instead of complaining, think of it as color for the story life is helping you build.

Accept the story. Be grateful for it. Then, use it to change the world.

#14

"When you learn to speak with influence, you open the door to many more opportunities than you realize."

— RK3

Have you ever been in a meeting or situation where you said nothing and lost an opportunity? If you're anything like me, you've had moments where you chose to be silent because you didn't feel you had anything groundbreaking to contribute.

Here's the kicker! Someone else says the very thing you were thinking and everyone treats them as if they had an amazing idea. Now, you shake your head because if only...

Research company, Vital Smarts, ran a test where they studied the correlation of delay in employees peaking up about a specific issue or idea and the estimated costs to a company. They found that when three days pass between the identification of a problem and an honest discussion about the issue, the company loses approximately $5,000. When the gap reaches 5 days, the company loses more than $25,000.

According to the same study
(https://www.prnewswire.com/ news-releases/long-silences-at-work-companies-struggle-when-employees-dont-quickly-surface-

problems-or-concerns-300679057.html), many people chose not to speak up for several reasons:

- some believed others wouldn't support their statements, leaving them socially isolated (45%)

- some expected retaliation of some sort from those who disagreed or may be impacted by their statements (46%)

- some didn't want to be labelled as complainers or contrarian (37%)

The bottom line for many is they don't want to stand out or stand alone. However, your words are less about you and more about the challenge in front of your audience.

I've been the person in the room, afraid to share their idea. And those experiences taught me three things:

1. It's not always about WHAT you have to say. It's about WHEN you say it and how relevant it is to the moment. However, you

don't know when that moment will appear so you must always take the chance.

2. The energy and passion you bring to your statements influences others to re-evaluate their own thoughts on the matter. Say it and say it with passion.

3. What you say is less about you and more about what your audience of that moment needs to hear. Take the focus off you and your fears. Instead, serve others with your words!

The world is just waiting to give you opportunities. You might feel you have to jump through hoops to receive them. They may even seem invisible or non-existent.

But they're there…waiting for you to grab them.

#15

"The two most powerful weapons in the world are the tongue and the pen."

— RK3

Some of the most famous people in history are speakers and writers. They became famous because of their uncanny ability to influence and make world-changing moments even after death. Maya Angelou, James Baldwin, Mahatma Gandhi, Socrates, Susan B. Anthony, William Shakespeare, Henry David Thoreau, and Charles Eastman are just a few of the incredible speakers and writers who impacted history. They didn't physically fight. They didn't look for TV programs to boost their fame. They didn't hire a team to craft clickbait articles to bring attention to their products. These influential people lived, wrote, and spoke with passion about their beliefs and values.

Many of us mute our voices because we are scared of the clapback.

"What if I speak up and people find out about my mistakes?"

"What if I open my mouth and someone says something critical about me?"

"Won't people point out my credentials if they don't like what I have to say?"

We fear our ability to make a difference. But what we fear more are the weapons we carry with us daily...our tongues and our minds. We have heard ourselves speaking negatively in our own minds and out of our mouths. So, we are intimately aware of the emotions and damage our words can cause. And so, we shy away. We make excuses. We blame our abilities or the lack of those abilities. Sometimes, our life experiences cause us to distance ourselves from our voice.

When Maya Angelou was just eight years old, she was raped by her mother's boyfriend. She found the courage to tell someone about this and even testified in court about it. But, after the court case, the boyfriend was found beaten to death, presumably by Maya's uncles. While it was never proven to be Maya's family members, she internalized this event as her fault. She thought his death came as a result of her words. In her book, I Know Why The Caged Bird Sings, she wrote, "I killed that man, because I told his name. And then I thought I would never speak again, because my voice would kill anyone." So, she stopped speaking for five years.

She was, however, an avid reader. One of her teachers became aware of this and coaxed her out of her self-imposed speech exile. One day while reading some poetry Maya had written, she stated, "Words mean more than what is set down on paper. It takes the human voice to infuse them with the shades of deeper meaning." These words seemed poetic to Maya and this teacher, Mrs. Flowers, eventually convinced Maya to begin reading some of her poetry aloud. Mrs. Flowers challenged Maya by telling her, "You don't begin to love poetry until you speak it."

Imagine a world without Maya's pen AND her voice.

No matter what language you speak or how well you did in school, you can speak or write to make a difference. Even if you have a physical obstacle limiting your ability, it's not impossible! It means a different effort and a different path.

Believe your ideas matter and will make a difference for someone. In many cases, that someone is you! Our ideas sometimes get stuck in our heads and bounce around endlessly until they finally lose steam. But when we allow them to come out into the light, they gain the ability to grow and magnify. You might think it insignificant. But, your idea, out in the world, has the power to change someone else's life.

This is your call and responsibility. Share the light. Share the power. Share it with your tongue and your pen.

#16

"Your words and influence will plant the seed of either success or failure in the mind of another."

– Napoleon Hill

Every word you say makes a difference. You may not realize it, but each word you utter changes something. Some shifts are significant, and some are small. But, every word adjusts energy, perspective, or response.

Some people realize this, and, as a result, choose to remain silent, fearing their words will create an unexpected result. Others embrace it, leverage it, and yield great results. We are born this way until the day we experience a negative response. Children, for the most part, are born, and sound is how they get our attention. Initially, they don't use words, but they use sound to let you know their needs and how they are feeling. Based on the response to their sounds, they use them repeatedly. Eventually, some of those verbal cues begin to morph into language. But how they learn and use language is groomed by the response they received to their sounds. Consistent negative responses create fear around the use of certain sounds, while persistent positive responses yield repeated use of those sounds.

We begin to recognize fear or permission quite early in life, and this determines much of the baseline activity for our voice. We start to lean into the positive responses more and automatically cringe when a negative response, real or imagined, is apparent. The challenge comes when we start to count the number of each response type subconsciously. When the negative responses begin to outnumber the positives, it becomes easier to choose a fear response, and this tends to become our baseline of operation. Much of this happens based on words said to us, around us, and about us.

Words create life and shape life. Words have energy and generate results. Is every result positive or easy? Absolutely not! But, the results we can experience are the ones we can address.

The day you realize how much influence you have is a pivotal day. For many, that day places weight on their shoulders, and they see it as a burden. But that special moment signals a shift from being trapped inside your head to recognizing the power you have over your surroundings. The moment a word leaves your lips, it has the power to create an emotional change in the life of another. Each word has power to plant seeds that can determine the path or destiny of someone else unless they themselves are strong enough to withstand the force. Every letter, every syllable carries unmistakable energy that can determine the future.

You already have the power. Now, you get to decide how you will use it. Find your voice! Embrace it and use it for good!

#17

"What is most important to me must be spoken, made verbal and shared, even at the risk of having it bruised or misunderstood."

– Audre Lorde

Have you ever had the experience of staying silent only to have someone raise their hand and share your idea? The worst part happens when the same idea gets cheered or receives accolades.

"That was brilliant. Why didn't we think of that earlier? Thanks, Jerry!"

"But, I did think of it earlier...I just didn't say anything because I was a bit nervous," you think to yourself.

I remember watching an episode of Key & Peele, a comedy sketch show, called High-Potenuse. The math teacher was explaining triangular measurement and mentioned the word hypotenuse. Upon hearing this word, one of the characters (Peele) whispered to the other (Key), "I wish I was high on potenuse." Key, surprised at the joke, laughed out loud and repeated the simple joke in his laughter. Once he repeated it, the entire class, including the teacher, exploded with laughter. Peele, seeing the laughter of the class, protested, letting them know the joke was his. The teacher scolded him for trying to take credit for something that was not his. However, the teacher thought the joke was hilarious, so when the principal stopped by, she asked Key to repeat the joke. The principal laughed and shared the anecdote with a comedian who happened to be at the school that day. The plot went on with the joke being shared so widely that Key got to meet the president of the United States to tell him the joke personally. At every turn, Peele protested, trying to get everyone to admit the original joke was his. But, no one would listen.

While the joke and the drug reference may be extreme, the situation is painfully familiar. We internalize our ideas. We passively share. Then, our jaws drop in shock and awe when we see the idea brought to life in another form or by someone else.

Why does this happen? Self-protection. We're scared of being hurt, getting judged, or being ridiculed. We don't want anyone to make us feel dumb. We're afraid of being the focus of laughter or finger-pointing. Sometimes, we have fear because we've been the ones pointing the finger and laughing. OUCH!

However, your ideas are important. They were divinely downloaded to you because God intended them to create change. He intended for them to open doors of brilliance. Your ideas initiate growth and reveal light. But the light is only revealed when the ideas are converted into words and released from their creative cocoon.

When a butterfly finally emerges from it's cocoon, it doesn't know what to expect. Sometimes, a predator may eat the butterfly. But most times, the butterfly emerges, flaps its wings, then flies off to provide beauty and pollinate flowers. Your words will pollinate, provide beauty, and create growth. But you must speak them, even at the risk of being misunderstood.

#18

"The most courageous act is still to think for yourself. Aloud."

– Coco Chanel

I admit it. I'm a recovering judger. I was judgmental. But I hid it in a disguise of being smart. I would discuss an idea with my friends and one person in the group would timidly say something different from the group. My mind...and sometimes my mouth...would say, "Why would you even say that? That makes no sense!" Sometimes, the person would recoil and say nothing else. My job was complete. Gavel dropped! Judgment executed!

Now, I shake my head as I realize I was the one who was close-minded and small. The courageous person was the one who was willing to think differently and say it out loud. It's easy to speak when you know everyone will agree.

You can be loud when you're confident no one will have a contrary opinion. But what about when they do? This is the essence of courage.

Many people feel threatened by things they don't understand or ideas that differ from their immediate value systems. When they feel the threat or tension, they fight against it and try to shut it down. I was guilty of this. In many cases, when you feel shut down, it's because your ideas force a new thought process and this is hard for most people.

Maybe you're in a meeting and disagree with an opinion shared by most others in the meeting. So, you remain quiet, or you say nothing else once they disagree with you.

Maybe you are a member of a project, and you find out there was a meeting to which you were not invited. Why not? You might be a threat to the group-think.

You hear all of the ideas presented, and you see a train-wreck coming, but instead of speaking up, you remain silent. You feel the tension in your body because you've been down this path before, and you instinctively know the answer. Yet, you say nothing, and you watch as the project derails.

We all have moments where we choose not to speak or we fear speaking. The decision is rooted in hurt and fear. This does nothing for the world. Change only happens through courage, courageous acts, and the willingness to speak up.

According to one perspective, life discourages you from courageous acts. Another view, the one I prefer, is that life gives you opportunities to practice courage. Sometimes, it starts with the simple willingness to own a different opinion and then share it aloud. This is more than just having an opposite view. It's the willingness to own an idea or perspective even when you're the only one who believes it.

This is courage! Be courageous!

#19

"You may not understand why you have experienced all you have until you put it all together in a story."

— RK3

In a commencement speech at Stanford University, Steve Jobs said, "You can only connect the dots going backwards." What did he mean? Picture yourself right now standing on a dot and looking out in front of you. Then imagine every moment, every experience in your life as a dot. Now, as you stand on your current dot, you don't see other dots in front of you. But, when you pick up your foot, a few dots appear. You get to choose which dot to step on. Some dots are close to you and other dots require you to jump to reach them. As you reach each dot, the other dot options disappear and only the ones you land on count.

There's no way for you to make sense of the dots going forward because they don't appear until you get to them. Some dots are easy. But, some dots are fire hot once you step on them. There are still more dots with nails and upside-down thumbtacks on them once your foot lands. Other dots are icy and cause you to feel unbalanced. Some dots are higher and even though they're right in front of you, you need a ladder to reach them.

None of these dots is the same. You don't know what dots will appear on the journey. However, at some point, you stop to take in where you are. You look back and see the dots behind you. Now, it makes sense and you see how each dot allowed you to reach your current dot. All together, you can tell a story with these dots.

It's easy to get caught up in the wind of life. Everything blends together and you don't stop long enough to look at the dots to recognize them for what they are...the experiences that create your life. Each dot holds a memory and an experience that has built you and created the picture of you.

Puzzle pieces on their own aren't clear. But they form a picture when you put them together.

You might be tempted to complain about the difficulty of your current dot. That's a waste of your time. Your complaint rarely, if ever, changes the existence of the dot. Instead, seek to understand how each dot contributes to the amazing story of you.

Now comes the important part. Tell the story!

#20

"Good communication, written or oral, begins with an understanding of the audience. If you can get inside their heads, you can find a way to connect."

– Debra Bennetts

The deepest human need is connection. When a speaker approaches the platform, the audience is begging for a bond. We desperately want the speaker to do well, but we also want them to connect with a deeper part of us that will respond. When asked to evaluate a presentation or talk, audience members will respond with some version of "I can't put my finger on it, but he/she just moved me."

The opposite response is a version of "The info was cool, but I just couldn't vibe with him/her." People crave connection and want us to reach their inner parts. They want us to sit on their internal park bench with them. They want to feel with us and through us. People want us to understand them.

So, when I craft a message, whether from the front of the room or in simple conversation, I ask myself, "what am I doing to connect intentionally?"

I want you to imagine a dinner table...one of the long, rectangular kind, with up to 12 people seated. You are speaking, but there is no sound. Yet, as you look around the table, you see heads thrown back in laughter, other heads laughing and nodding in agreement, and others struggling to get the next bite into their mouths through their laughter. All eyes are focused on you and waiting for your next statement. This is attention, intention, and connection. Words are great, but randomly put together, they don't create an experience. And, the purpose of the experiential word sequencing is to remind the audience of a time when they have had a similar experience.

One of the best ways to create a connection is through story. When you tell a story, people imagine themselves in your story and, in many cases, substitute themselves as the main character. They ride with you through the hills and valleys of the story. They take the scenic route with you because they're all-in.

Humans are built for empathic response and connection. So, my communication goal is to seek the best way to access this. Ask a question. Get them to imagine. Invite them into your story.

When you find your voice and share your story, you open an inner pathway to what the human heart craves.

#21

"It only takes one voice, at the right pitch, to start an avalanche."

– Diana Hardy

Susan was a brilliant writer looking to make a name for herself in the journalism industry. Every article she wrote was thought-provoking and inspiring. There was only one problem. Susan refused to share the articles with people who could publish them. She desperately wanted to be a journalist but was afraid of doing the one thing she needed to do...write in public.

In a conversation with her mentor, he found Susan had a crippling case of "impostor syndrome." She was afraid no one would listen to her or take her seriously. As an unpublished writer, she felt she had no credibility. "Well, outside of publishing, what's your plan to get there," her mentor asked.

There are a lot of Susan's, in our world. In fact, the International Journal of Behavioral Science lists a study where it finds more than 70% of people experience impostor syndrome at some point in their lives. This is the nagging idea that somehow, you don't belong or deserve to be where you are. Impostor phenomenon would have you believe you don't deserve to be heard because you have nothing important enough to say.

We watch as others say what they want, and our gut tells us to speak. But, like Susan, we don't feel smart enough or important enough. And so, instead, you say nothing. I say nothing. Susan says nothing.

We want someone to hear us, but it seems futile to shout. We want to stand out, but there is a sea of noise, distraction, and Snapchat filters.

However, standing out isn't required. It isn't always necessary to be the loudest, most controversial, or most dramatic. Although it seems counterintuitive, standing out requires speaking at the right time and the correct pitch. But, you won't know the right time or pitch unless you happen to be speaking. There is no light bulb moment, flash or start button. You must be in the game. You don't need to be loud all the time. Instead, be on the mountain.

SPEAK! Start an AVALANCHE!

#22

"You don't have to change who you are, you have to become more of who you are."

– Sally Hogshead

You're already amazing! The problem is you may not believe it. Negative images and auditory messages bombard you and make you believe the opposite is true. These messages make amazing seem impossible. You may not pay attention to them but the 'little villain' in your brain is paying attention and repeating them when you aren't conscious.

Most people allow the 'little villain' free reign so he runs roughshod through our brains saying whatever the heck he wants. And they're lies. Lies are his specialty. His lies aim to minimize you, discourage you and sap every ounce of power from you.

He tells you that to gain success, you must change everything. Then, he casually mentions how hard it'll be to make the necessary changes.

Well, here's some good news. The villain is wrong. You don't have to change everything. You just need to focus on the greatness. It already exists inside you. I know because you already do some things well. Maybe you're a great cook. Or, you're very hospitable. You make people laugh without thinking about it. You might even be a problem solver. There's something inside you that other people admire. And it's time for you to do more of it. Today is your day to access your personal superpower! When you access it, put it to work now because that's how you weaken the 'little villain.'

Successful action weakens the villain even if those successes are small. Recognize them, string them together and show the 'villain' your greatness.

The world needs you to come out of hiding!

#23

"You have to expect things of yourself before you can do them."

– Michael Jordan

How high do you want to climb? Are you satisfied with where you are, or do you want more? Some years ago, I had an interaction with a potential coaching client. We were discussing goals, and I asked a question about his end game.

"I just want to get to a point where I'm comfortable." was his response.

I pushed a bit further by asking, "What does comfortable look like for you?"

"Well, you know. Everything is paid, and I'm good!"

We continued the conversation, and he finally admitted what he wanted...wealth. But, he wasn't comfortable with being wealthy because he grew up hearing wealthy people were evil. So, he carried this baggage with him for years, and whenever his business got to a place where it might grow, he would, unintentionally, sabotage it.

As a result, he would set low expectations. As he got closer to these low expectations, he would sabotage because exceeding them meant a new level of growth. Yet, somewhere deep in his mind, he wanted to be seen as successful.

I wish my prospective client were the only person who carried out this behavior. Unfortunately, many of us do the same thing. It may not be with a business or a job. But, it may be with a relationship or with a dream. Experiences we have early in life frame many of the choices we make or the limits we place on ourselves. If we grow up seeing risk-taking celebrated, then our pain threshold for risk is much higher. This doesn't always mean our dreams automatically become smaller. And, here lies the conflict. When a big idea comes in close proximity to a low risk-threshold, self-sabotage is sure to follow. The dream burns and makes you uncomfortable, but any indication of accomplishment causes an aversion reflex, and you go running back or break something on purpose to return to the comfort zone.

When it feels like your ideas may cause rejection, you temper them with softer words. Instead of saying, "This is the most effective path based on the info we have," or "This is something that will work for us," we add 'in my opinion' to the end of the sentence just in case someone challenges. We add qualifiers to our language because we are nervous about appearing too authoritative, or we are scared of the magnitude of our ideas.

However, it's time to find your voice and embrace your dream language. If you want to reach higher, you must EXPECT higher! If you EXPECT low, chances are you'll match it. If you EXPECT high, chances are you'll match it! Others will set expectations for you if you let them. So, why not set them for yourself! Then, DO THEM!

#24

"The most powerful people in the world have learned the power of communication."

— RK3

According to Warren Buffett, the 3rd richest man in the world, the most important skill he learned was the skill of communication and public speaking. You can have the most fabulous idea in the world. However, if you're unable to effectively transfer those ideas to others in a way they can understand and get excited about, then you have an unfruitful idea.

Imagine having a picture in your head and never being able to draw it. I remember having comic book competitions with my brother when I was young. He was a natural artist. But, I had to work hard at it. He drew great pictures with ease, but I had to find an actual comic book. Then I would trace the superhero pictures several times before attempting to draw it in my own comic book. I knew how I wanted it to LOOK. It just took work to translate the right image through my fingers.

Imagine having a story in your brain and never being able to write it. For some, this shows up as writers' block. The big picture idea is in your head but you don't know how exactly to put it into words. It's frustrating, and it can emotionally wear you down.

Imagine planting a seed in the ground and never seeing the stem break the surface. As a child in Jamaica, I remember taking a seed my dad gave me and planting it in the ground. I watered it and expected the seed to spring up immediately. Every day, for a week, I would water the seed. Then, I lay on the ground to see if anything was growing. Nothing. After a week, I figured nothing was going to happen, so I stopped watering and visiting the seed. One day nearly two weeks later, I was playing and noticed a green leaf and stem coming up out of the ground right where I had planted my seed. I'd given up on the seed, but the watering and the nutrients in the ground caused the growth.

Our ideas are potent seeds that we must water and share for them to be useful. When we revisit the idea, turn it around and play with it in our minds, this is the water. But, when we share it with others and begin acting on it, this is the fertile ground that causes growth.

When you develop the skill of speaking, that's the water. The day you begin to tell your story is the day your idea becomes useful. This is why you must find your voice. If an apple seed is never planted and watered, then it's just a seed. When you plant, water it and develop it, you can feed a village.

"But other people have seeds. They don't need mine to survive!", you might say.

Just as lactose-intolerant humans need options, your fruit is the option needed to feed the progress of someone specific. Don't rob them. Feed them! Use your voice and share your story!

#25

"Noble and great. Courageous and determined. Faithful and fearless. That is who you are and who you have always been. And understanding it can change your life, because this knowledge carries a confidence that cannot be duplicated any other way."

– Sherri Dew

Remember the day when you propped yourself up and decided you were going to walk? No? I'll bet it was a long time ago. You may not remember, but there was something special about that day. Risk and possibility filled each moment. As you pushed yourself up, you took the huge risk you were going to fall and bang your head against a nearby object or the floor. And, it was also possible you were going to propel yourself far enough forward to take a step or two...maybe even three.

You risked falling forward and busting your lip. Yet, there was also the possibility of finding your balance.

If you could replay the video from that day, you might see grown-ups hovering over you, eyes wide with anticipation; faces rippled with excitement and arms ready to catch you. Or, maybe you caught the adults by surprise. But, the look on your face, the excitement, and anticipation of the moment clearly showed through your determined smile.

You may not remember the day, but it was a courageous day. You were determined to achieve something, and nothing was going to stop you. That's who you are. That's your core. You weren't built with the fears you have now. You were made to recognize and operate in possibility. And yet, something happened along the way and caused you to wither away from your inner amazing-ness. What was it? Maybe you aren't clear about what it was. Or, perhaps you think about the moment all the time...the moment that stripped away all of your confidence and your courage.

It seems like that, at least. But, you are full of courage and confidence.

Your next level begins with you believing that. The next step towards finding and owning your voice is the moment you recognize you can recapture your courage.

When you remember that, you begin to own your day. Your voice wasn't meant to be silent. You were meant to impact the world and shift its operation. You were built to propel yourself and others towards greater heights.

Understand this and embrace it. You were not created to fear. You were faithful first! Own it!

#26

"The tongue can paint what the eye can't see."

– Chinese Proverb

"Imagine what it would be like if every time you walked into a room, everyone looked up at you and smiled the broadest smile you'd ever seen."

I began my keynote with those words, and immediately, I could see heads tilt to the side, creating the picture in their minds. I could see the smiles and the warm feeling of affirmation sweep over the room as everyone envisioned their own version of being the guest of honor. I did my job! We could have stopped then. But, I wanted to start a video in their brains.

Remember the last movie you loved? It was more than just a visual experience. You connected with it and felt something special when you watched it. Maybe your eyes welled up a bit, and you did everything you could to keep the water from flowing out of them. Or, perhaps, your heart began to race and skipped a beat or two every time a twist came.

I didn't want the audience to hear me. Instead, I wanted them to experience nostalgia, internal emotional replay and then...only then, did I want them to experience me. More accurately, I wanted my audience to experience WITH me.

My words were important. But, when I left the stage, I wanted to leave them inspired and reflective. The best way for me to do that was to allow them to create their own room. The color was up to them. The decor was whatever they wanted it to be. They could choose who they wanted to be in that room. Because the audience members could make all of these decisions in just a moment, they owned the picture.

A picture is worth a thousand words, but just a few words can paint an unforgettable picture. When you speak, instead of focusing on your words, focus on the image you want the audience to see. Direct them to use their mind's eye. Permit them to reaccess child-like imagination. Lead them towards a mental vacation.

Use words or phrases like 'imagine,' 'what if,' 'reflect,' 'Just think about,' 'see with me,' or 'envision.'

You can use your voice to help guide people, if only for a moment, out of their own stress-built world and into what could be.

Paint a picture with your tongue

#27

"The world suffers not because of the violence of bad people but because of the silence of good people."

– Unknown

Guilty! Guilty! Guilty! No, this isn't the proclamation of a court judge. This is my personal admission. Unfortunately, I've been silent in moments where my voice could have made a difference.

Have you experienced this? Do you remember moments where you KNOW you could have spoken up? As a teen growing up in New York City, I saw "boyfriends" mistreating "girlfriends" on the subway. Because I was young and scared of getting involved, I said nothing and switched train cars. Mind your business and stay alive. This was the mentality. And, it probably is sound advice because there are stories of 'good samaritans' paying the price for their involvement. I wanted to make it home. So, I followed the advice that made sense to me as a kid. Still, I was silent.

I wish I could blame it on being young and not knowing better. But, as an adult, I've been in rooms where someone was attacked, and I did nothing. In some cases, I was guilty of joining the attack. As violent words of gossip and laughter flew back and forth, I could feel my heart pinch. I knew it wasn't right. But, I continued because I didn't want to stand up. I was afraid.

What was I afraid of? Maybe the same thing you have been fearful of also. I was scared of being criticized. I didn't want the pendulum of anger to swing in my direction suddenly. The same arrows being thrown at someone else could hurt me.

It's funny how we can watch a news channel and shake our heads at the behavior of criminals who hurt others with guns and other weapons. Yet, we use our tongues to cause more pain. The hurt occurs when we slander, but it also happens when we remain silent in the face of an opportunity to lift, encourage, and empower.

It isn't easy to speak up. When you expect pushback or conflict, it's hard to open your mouth to advocate for someone else. But, the world gets worse when bad behavior is unchecked. Silence is acceptance...acceptance borne out of fear. So, silence is giving in to fear rather than owning courage.

You have a voice. What do you want to do with it? Will you be silent and allow shady behavior to continue? Or will you speak and let light shine?

#28

"Our lives begin to end the day we become silent about the things that matter."

– Martin Luther King, Jr.

Your voice matters! You don't need to yell and scream about everything. But, your voice is essential. You're the reason I wrote this book. I'm convinced you have a story that'll make a difference in someone's life. Why am I so convinced? You're reading this.

I remember moments when I thought my story wasn't important enough. It wasn't dramatic enough. There were no heart-stopping scenes, miraculous recoveries, or car chases (well, there was that one time). I was born with both my arms. My parents were alive, healthy, and at home. When I looked around me, I saw nothing but blessings. Why would I appear credible to ANYONE when talking about pain, doubt, insecurities, esteem, or purpose? I thought no one would listen because my story didn't have a massive climax with Michael Bay explosions and Jackie Chan action sequences.

I was wrong. After speaking at a conference, an attendee came up and shared how she felt I intended my story "just for her." I had shared what I call my signature story. Without detailing the entire speech here, I shared how I became silenced as a child through simple circumstances and yet grew up to become a speaker who teaches people about speaking and using their voices. I realized something. My usual was her dramatic. The moments I took for granted seemed amazing to her. The experiences I sailed through seemed like her dream.

As she spoke, her eyes welled with tears. At that moment, she made a commitment. She would no longer delay her dreams. She was going to "get after them."

My words mattered...to her. My voice mattered...to her. And, even if she was the only person I could ever touch, she was still the reason for my voice.

Now, it's your turn. Find your voice...because, your words matter...to someone!

Speak Up! Speak out! Live!

Conclusion

Sharing your experience is difficult. When you read social media or turn on the TV, it can feel like the whole world is watching and waiting to make fun of your failures. During the US Presidential election in 2016, I remember feeling more than ever like the keyboard warriors were out. When someone shared an opinion, it wasn't just heavily scrutinized. There were personal vicious attacks. It felt like compassion and understanding were out the window.

I remember being "forced" to watch an episode of one of the Real Housewives shows. I don't know which state or which area. But, I remember feeling like the flaws, criticism, judgment, and drama were what drove the show. Although this was a TV show, it wasn't much different than some of the drama I was seeing online.

Life seems like it's become a TV show where ratings are driven by dramatic, negative, and wild scenes. So, it's an easy jump to understand how we can feel judged the moment we walk out of our safe zones. I get it! You're nervous about putting yourself on a poster board where anyone can throw darts and arrows.

For years, I felt like I had to be perfect. I suppose that's part of the process when you grow up as a preacher's kid. I felt enormous pressure to do things the "right way." So, when I failed my Organic Chemistry class in college, I didn't see it as a story I could share with the world. It just felt like an anvil on a chain around my neck. This secret would have to be buried. Or, when I began my Masters program and hated it so much I quit going to class. I couldn't tell anyone because I would be judged and brought up in front of "the council" to be embarrassed, right?

We tell ourselves stories daily. And because it's our voice, we tend to believe those stories and hold them tightly. But, what if you could shift the story in your head? What if the story you told was no longer a weight but a launchpad? What if your story was the thing you stood on to see higher and reach further?

Guess what? It is! You can use it now. There's only one requirement. You must TELL IT!

A hidden story is like a brick weighing you down. But a revealed story is like a sail carrying you, and anyone who hears it, through rough waters into newly discovered land.

I encourage you to go back through this book to find the quote that inspires you to ACTION most. Then, go to www.robertkennedy3.com/findyourvoice to let me know in the comments there. If you have another amazing quote to share, post it there as well.

ADDITIONAL ACTIONS TO HELP YOU FIND YOUR VOICE

1. ACTION: Make a list of 5 skills you learned as a child. Write down the steps used to learn the skill. This is something you can teach.

2. ACTION: Make a list of 5 people who are helping you grow personally. Contact each of them to ask who else they might recommend you contact to help with your personal growth.

3. ACTION: Schedule a 1-hour slot on your personal calendar. Write your greatest challenge and how you have overcome it. (Everyone has a challenge they've overcome even if it seems small)

4. ACTION: Find a school, church, local organization that'll allow you to deliver a 15-30 minute talk about your life or personal story.

5. ACTION: If you're on social media, choose a time where you can share your story in a live video for 10-15 minutes. Then, invite others to share theirs too. This may be a starting point for your own online community.

ADDITIONAL RESOURCES

SPEAKING WITH CONFIDENCE MINI-COURSE
Learn a simple framework that'll allow you to
speak with confidence, power and without notes.
www.storytellersgrowthlab.com/speakwithconfide
nceminicourse

ZERO TO PAID
SELF-PACED COURSE
Learn the actions, resources and materials
necessary to go from dreaming of speaking to
getting paid for speaking.
www.storytellersgrowthlab.com/zerotopaidcourse

JOIN THE COMMUNITY
I want to help you with your stories. So, I invite you
to join me in the Storytellers Growth Lab. Join by
going to www.storytellersgrowthlab.com